god forgotten face

Robin Maddock

TROLLEY

A POEM IS A CITY

a poem is a city filled with streets and sewers
filled with saints, heroes, beggars, madmen,
filled with banality and booze,
filled with rain and thunder and periods of
drought, a poem is a city at war,
a poem is a city asking a clock why,
a poem is a city burning,
a poem is a city under guns
its barbershops filled with cynical drunks,
a poem is a city where God rides naked
through the streets like Lady Godiva,
where dogs bark at night, and chase away
the flag; a poem is a city of poets,
most of them quite similar
and envious and bitter...
a poem is this city now,
50 miles from nowhere,
9:09 in the morning,
the taste of liquor and cigarettes,
no police, no lovers, walking the streets,
this poem, this city, closing its doors,
barricaded, almost empty,
mournful without tears, aging without pity,
the hardrock mountains,
the ocean like a lavender flame,
a moon destitute of greatness,
a small music from broken windows...

a poem is a city, a poem is a nation,
a poem is the world...

and now I stick this under glass
for the mad editor's scrutiny,
the night is elsewhere
and faint gray ladies stand in line,
dog follows dog to estuary,
the trumpets bring on gallows
as small men rant at things
they cannot do

Charles Bukowski

to Plymouth
and
the kindness
of its Strangers

also for and against Bianca

Resurgam

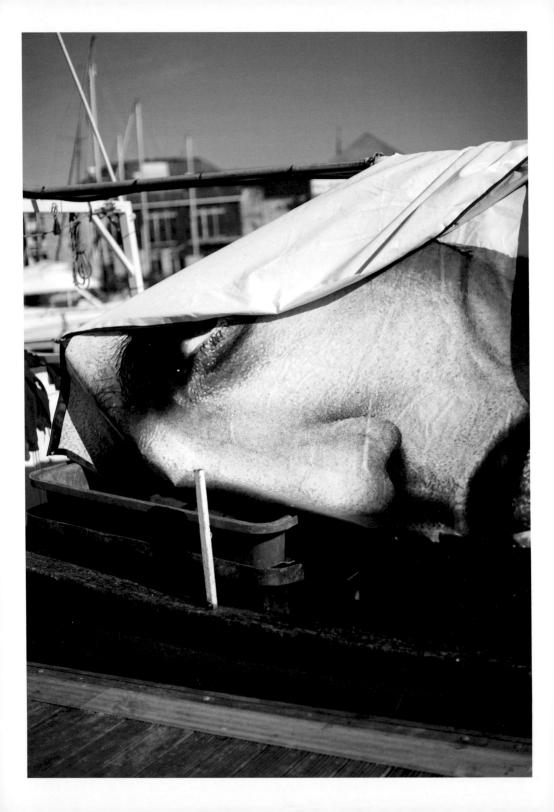

41 churches
100 pubs
10,000 photographs
26 Schools
7,200 books
336 people
and when
it was all over
they song

CORNISH
PASTIES IN
EU VICTORY

Hollywood
Legend
to film
on DARTMOOR

CITY CHILD
POVERTY Shock

Sickening
Blow KILLED
Footballer

TAXI TYCOON
ON $60 A week

MAN
HARASSES EX
WITH 29,000
CALLS & TEXTS

GAMES ADDICT
KID

WORST DEFEAT
in 16 Years

WOMAN USES
child 8 to
Steal

Haunted by Mum's
Murder

SADISTIC
SAVAGE
AND EVIL

MAN IN
400FT DEATH
PLUNGE

HUNT for
OWNER OF
£1M LOTTERY
TICKET

END THIS
ARGYLE
MADNESS

2 4 1
KFC
DEALS

Grandma
had nylon bed sheets
all snagging toes
electric charges
you can't believe
in the future
much more than that

the fighting stops
as the National anthem
plays on the jukebox
as the queen must
be saluted.

So my wife
runs off with
my best friend
if you touch my
fishing gear
your dead
did he have a bigger
Rod then?

my uncle
7ft Tall
20 inch neck
used to
Run around
the field
with a young horse
on his shoulders
Just
to make us laugh

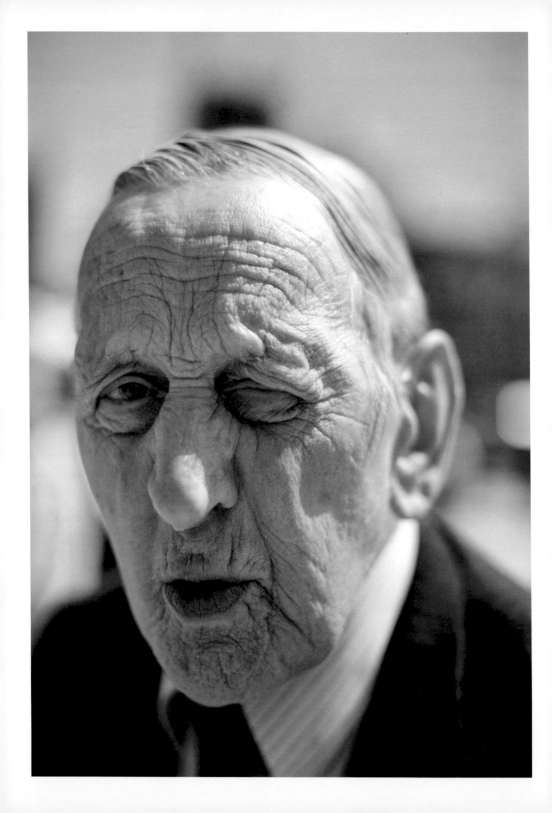

shop online at www.houseoffraser.co.uk

devonport gozon
gentle men
in a world gone hollyoaks
everyone's fully pumped

RECYCLABLES

City of
Plymouth

on our first date
getting cosh out
you're old
but
you're hot
guy behind
you'll need a lot
more than that mate

I won't pull
tonight
I mean
As it STANDS
I mean
AS IT STANDS

we make boats
for wealthy people
we can't be seen
in a book
with prostitutes

Frankie Howard
I'm about 7
The Palace
was a palace
now
night of the long knives
I look down on this

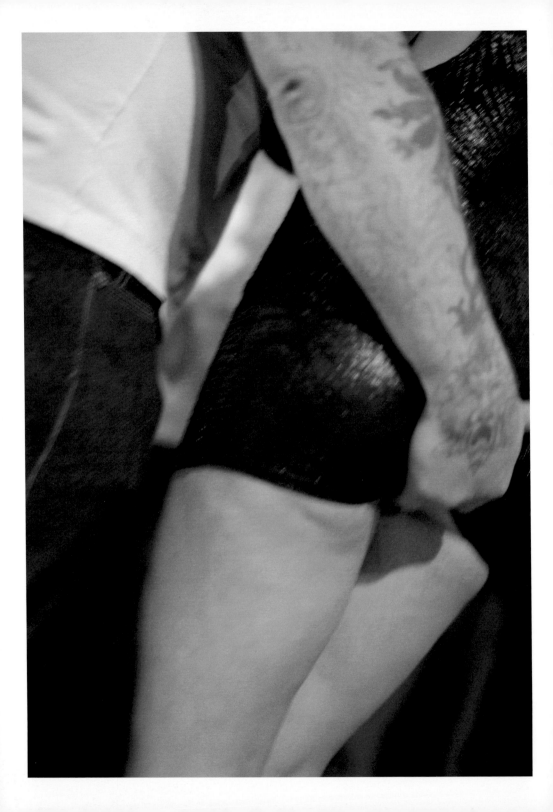

here
I Sink
and
disappear
like a Rat
up a drainpipe

on union St
over a spill of pits
I met plymouth
in the heart of
a busted prophet

at Delphi
in the ruins of a beginning
it still says in stone
know thy self

In Praise of Blitzed Cities

Owen Hatherley

The bombed cities are all different, but they all have a similar feeling. That doesn't mean they're homogeneous, far from it, but that the loss at their heart is alike, if often different in scale. On the far more brutally fought Eastern front, there are several cities where only a tiny, or even non-existent proportion of the population can trace their families' presence there further back than the late 1940s. Cities that were wiped out, like Warsaw; cities where an entire population was removed and another population resettled there, like Wrocław, Kaliningrad, Lviv. Yet in many of the bombed cities, you feel like this has taken place, even when it hasn't – like the entire city was vacated and resettled with a whole other group of people with entirely different values and different ways of seeing the world. Sometimes, in the more grandiose of the Blitzed cities, along the walkways of Sheffield or Thamesmead, you feel something even harsher – that this new city was built by some race of giants that disappeared, leaving us to a landscape too big, too dramatic, too confident, for such simple folk as us. Whichever way the question is posed, the bombed cities still, even now, sixty years later, feel alien to many people.

They're incoherent, they're strange, they're dramatic, they're modern, they're messy, they're not 'historic', except for the odd little reconstructed reservation – a Barbican, a Stare Miasto. This is their strength. In the European cities that the Luftwaffe or the RAF didn't do over, you have a 19th century centre ringed by post-war housing, a clear divide between one and the other, which curdled over the decades into a strict spatial divide between one sort of people and another sort of people. In the bombed cities, we don't have that – we have council flats next to Regency terraces next to parks conjured up from bomb sites. The super-rich sleep slightly less easily in their beds, erecting gates around their new developments to reflect how unsafe they feel. Tourists shun the new places, all 'concrete jungles' and 'monstrous carbuncles'. In the process, these forgotten cities have some of the strongest, and strangest identities in the UK.

I say 'we' in all this, I at least partly mean 'I'. When growing up in the levelled port of Southampton in the 1990s, time felt out of joint. Tall, ultramodern constructions were being knocked down, brick simulations of Victorian streets that never existed were built in their place. It took years before the age of things could be easily ascertained, before I realised that the future was over before I was born; but I was hardly alone in this. So what all of us did, living there, was use the loathed public spaces for loitering – we'd hang around in the precincts, drink cider in the civic amenities, like greasier, pimplier versions of the attenuated watercolour peopleoids that populated the drawings of 1940s planners. The plazas were ringed with charity shops, and it seemed oddly just and fitting – the worn elegance of the post-war city making a dignified withdrawal from the screeching crassness of the giant, exurban American malls. But there was another, double absence, where the future did continue in a disavowed form – in the almost hidden grandeur of the container port, the gigantic automated spectacle of cranes, tracks and multicoloured boxes that somehow we all conspired not to look at. Living in a port supposedly meant the nautical tourism that filled the derelict docks, the reminiscence over the days when sailors actually got off the boat, not this awesome robotic spectacle with its practically invisible workers.

This sense that the post-war city can't be 'seen' properly, that it is somehow outside of our normal time and space at the same time as being completely mundane and ordinary, is at its most vivid in post-war Plymouth. Ask many people about Plymouth and the immediate response will almost certainly be negative and almost certainly involve the word 'concrete'. Irrespective of the qualities or otherwise of that material, most of post-war Plymouth wasn't made from it – nor was it even particularly modernist, with most of it redesigned on a grand, European scale, with a wide central boulevard, a grid plan and ornamented, expensive, if somewhat severe stone buildings filling up what space wasn't left open. In fact, as bombed cities go, Plymouth is less an asymmetrical, multilevel modernist Coventry or Sheffield than a neoclassical, imperial Warsaw or (East) Berlin, albeit on a much reduced scale. Spaces like this, with their long, straight, wide roads lined with symmetrical, civic buildings, always feel ceremonial, designed not so much for mundane use as for something else, something a little more regimented; spaces for celebrations, or as some would no doubt have it, military parades - this is a garrison town after all. Obviously we don't march down them, and even if we wanted to, the spaces have been so filled of late with everything from gardens to funfairs to giant TVs that it would be fairly impossible. But the sense is still there – behind the grime and the adverts you can find a grandeur that reveals what is really hated about this place – it got ideas above its station.

The Blitzed twentieth century ports always suffer from a double loss. First of the pre-Blitz streetscape (thanks to the wonders of modern technology, specifically photography, we can gaze longingly at the Georgian buildings destroyed by the bombers and the planners, something the Georgians weren't able to do when they destroyed thousands of medieval and Elizabethan buildings). Second, of the port itself, which has either literally disappeared or transformed into something mechanised, that leaves no trace, with no salty sea dog seedy glamour except in the maritime museums. A third loss is only just slowly starting to be registered – the loss of the socialist spirit that impelled us to redesign our chaotic, profiteering cities as something unified, public and civic, without gates, fences or hierarchies.

All this might make Plymouth sound like a melancholic place, even a grim one. It isn't. The Blitzed cities are poor, of course they are – but they share a shabby, ad hoc vitality that most heritage cities would die for (if they're lucky enough still to be living). What we need to do now is reclaim them, to take possession of the Socialist city of the 1950s for ourselves, as the little gang of Goths embracing on the precinct do in these photographs. After we've done that, we'll have the confidence to build anew.

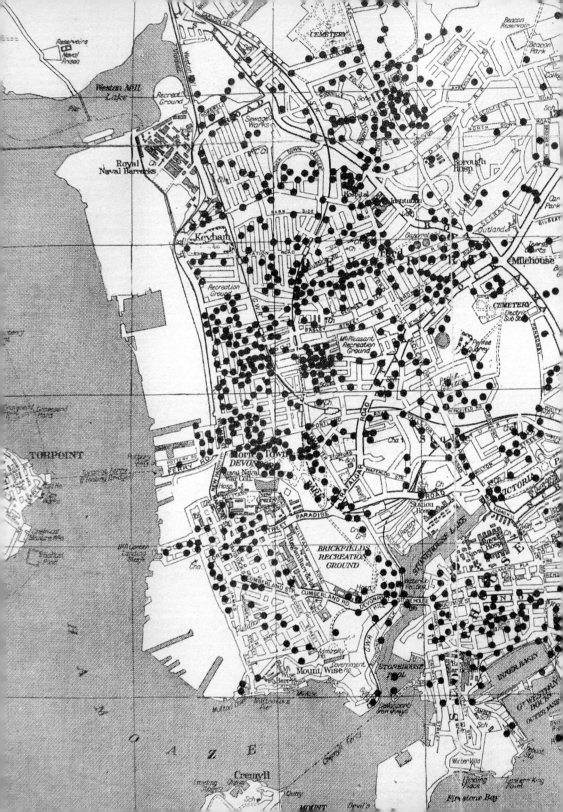

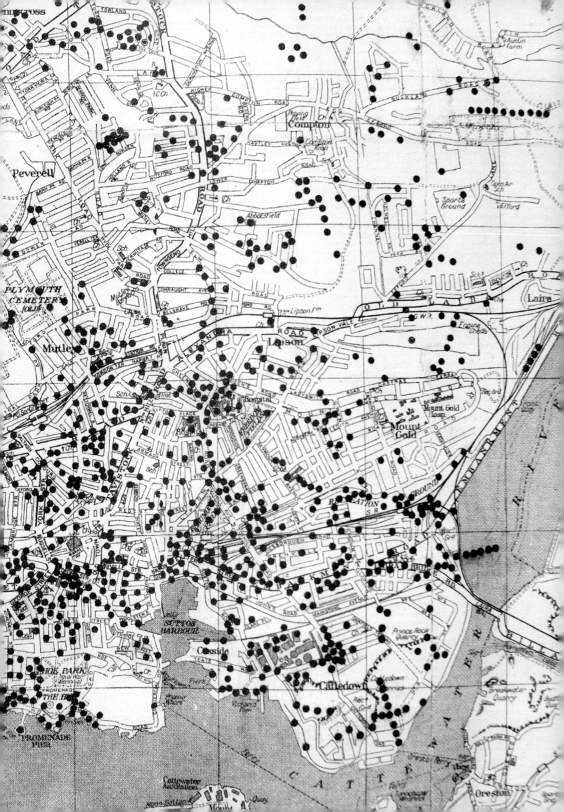

Thanks to...

for wonderful trust and help in Plymouth...

Wendy Smith at Babcock ltd
Anne-Marie Clark at TR2
Agnes at Plymfed
Chris Arscott at the Royal South Western Sailing Club
Charles Howeson at the PABC
Liz at Council House
Wildman Chris
Lambert and lads at Devonport Gym
Councillor Tina Touy
The Halcyon Centre staff in North Prospect
Velma the angel card reader
Mike Howells a proper artist
All the staff at Plymouth Trawler Agents especially Alison.

Chris Ellis for Digital Post Production

For true friendships, inspiration & shelter from mid-price hotels during
the making of this book...

Ruby & Aya Quince and
Jordan, Tara & Mads Grant

Thanks for being brilliant
Gigi and Hannah with the making again
Simon Bainbridge for floating an idea years ago
My parents for setting a standard
Adam Green and PJ Harvey for musical substance
Owen for the great words
Larkin via Hannah for the title
My bro for still energising me

Published in Great Britain in 2011
by Trolley Ltd

www.trolleybooks.com

ISBN 978-1-907112-34-8

Printed in Italy 2011 by Grafiche Antiga
© All rights reserved, 2011

Photographs © Robin Maddock
Text © Charles Bukowski, Owen Hatherley
Design Fruitmachine